The Greatest Financial Scandals of the Last Twenty Years: From Madoff to the Cover up of the OptionSellers/INT FCStone Scandal

The most famous financial scandal of the last twenty years was the Bernie Madoff scandal of 2008. There have been more than a dozen books written about it. One of the best was "Too Good to Be True," by Erin Arvidlund of the Philadelphia Inquirer. Madoff paid dearly, and is serving a 145-year jail sentence. The only good news is that recently the investors recovered the $19 billion he had taken from them. This did not include the pumped up profits that Madoff claimed he had earned. Madoff is currently petitioning to have his sentence commuted. He has paid a huge price for his misdeeds, including seeing his son commit suicide.

THE WASTE MANAGEMENT SCANDAL OF 1998

The Madoff scandal was not the first major financial scandal. The first was the Waste Management Scandal of 1998. A few highlights from that scandal include:

- Company: Houston-based publicly traded waste management company

- What happened: The Corporation reported $1.7 billion in fake earnings

- The main players: Founder/Chief Executive Officer/Chairman Dean L. Buntrock and other top executives; Arthur Andersen Company (auditors)

- How they did it: The company allegedly falsely increased the depreciation time for their property, plant, and equipment on the balance sheets.

- How they got caught: A new CEO and management team went through the books

- Penalties: Settled a shareholder class-action suit for $457 million. SEC fined Arthur Andersen $7 million

- Interesting fact: After the scandal, new CEO A. Maurice Meyers set up an anonymous company hotline where employees could report dishonest or improper behavior

The next major scandal was the **Enron scandal of 2001.** Below are the highlights:

- Enron was a Houston-based commodities, energy, and service corporation

- What happened: Shareholders lost $74 billion, thousands of employees and investors lost their retirement accounts, and many employees lost their jobs

- Main players: CEO Jeff Skilling and former CEO Ken Lay

- How they did it: Kept huge debts off balance sheets

- How they got caught: Turned in by internal whistleblower Sherron Watkins; high stock prices fueled external suspicions

- Penalties: Lay died before serving time; Skilling got 24 years in prison. The company filed for bankruptcy. Arthur Andersen was found guilty of fudging Enron's accounts

- Amazing fact: Fortune Magazine named Enron "America's Most Innovative Company" six years in a row prior to the scandal

WORLDCOM SCANDAL (2002)

Enron was a telecommunications company that is now MCI, Inc.

- What happened: Inflated assets by as much as $11 billion, leading to 30,000 lost jobs and $180 billion in losses for investors

- Main player: CEO Bernie Ebbers

- How he did it: Underreported line costs by capitalizing rather than expense them and he inflated revenues with fake accounting entries

- How he got caught: WorldCom's internal auditing department uncovered $3.8 billion of fraud

- Penalties: CFO was fired, controller "resigned", and the company filed for bankruptcy. Ebbers was sentenced to 25 years for fraud, conspiracy, and filing false documents with regulators

- The most important result came within weeks of the scandal. Congress passed the Sarbanes-Oxley Act, introducing the most sweeping set of new business regulations since the 1930s.

The WorldCom scandal was, until the schemes came to light in 2008, the largest accounting scandal in history. Ebbers is currently serving a twenty-five year prison term at the, in Texas. In 2013, and named Ebbers as the fifth-worst CEO in American history. In 2009, CNBC named him the tenth most corrupt CEO of all time. If there is one theme to rival the terrorism of 9-11 that occurred twenty years ago it would have to be corporate greed and malfeasance. Many of the biggest corporate accounting scandals in history happened during that time.

What happened: Inflated assets by as much as $11 billion, leading to 30,000 lost jobs and $180 billion in losses for investors.

Main player: CEO Bernie Ebbers

How he did it: Underreported line costs by capitalizing rather than expensing and inflated revenues with fake accounting entries.

How he got caught: WorldCom's internal auditing department uncovered $3.8 billion of fraud.

Penalties: CFO was fired, controller resigned, and the company filed for bankruptcy. Ebbers sentenced to 25 years for fraud, conspiracy and filing false documents with regulators.

Within weeks of the scandal, Congress passed the Sarbanes-Oxley Act, introducing the most sweeping set of new business regulations.

THE TYCO SCANDAL WAS

THE LONGEST RUNNING THEFT:

The Tyco International scandal refers to the 2002 theft by former company CEO and Chairman Dennis Kozlowski and former corporate Chief Financial Officer Mark Swartz of as much as $600 million from the firm. The scandal turned into a long, drawn out trial as the two accused men vigorously denied any wrongdoing and fought the charges vehemently. In their March 2004 trial, they argued strenuously that the then-Board of Directors of Tyco had authorized the questionable $150 million they had received as compensation for services rendered. The trial ended in mistrial and a retrial occurred in 2005. At this second trial, they were both declared guilty of more than thirty individual corporate violations.

The first trial ended in a mistrial because of a suspicious incident that happened during the final jury deliberations. Juror Ruth Jordan made an "okay" sign on the defense table as she passed through the courtroom. While she insisted that had not been the gesture she made, the publicity of the incident by the *Journal* led many people to believe it had been a set up for the defendants. Judge Michael Obus declared a mistrial over the incident in 2004.

In the jury verdict of the second trial on the Tyco International scandal in 2005, Kozlowski and Swartz received convictions on all but one of the over thirty counts leveled against them. The verdicts brought possible jail times for as many as twenty-five years in state level incarceration. Kozlowski received a minimum of eight years and four months of jail time, with a possible maximum sentence of twenty-five. Swartz received the exact same sentence for his role in the Tyco International scandal.

A class action lawsuit followed the Tyco International scandal criminal trial with a verdict handed down by Federal District Court Judge Paul Barbadoro in May of 2007. Tyco consented to pay out $2.92 billion to a group of the cheated victims. Their corporate auditors, Pricewaterhouse Coopers, also agreed to pay $225 million in damages to the injured.

Unfortunately, I was the victim of a more recent scandal, the OptionSellers/INT FCStone scandal that erupted in the second week in November 2018. This scandal was under the Jurisdiction of the Commodity Futures Trading Commission (CFTC) rather than the SEC. If it were under the purview of the SEC, someone would already be in jail.

For me, it is very personal. As a young General Counsel and Staff Director of the Senate Agriculture Committee, I drafted the Commodity Futures Trading Commission Act of 1974. This was the authorizing legislation for the new CFTC. I was only the draftsman.

The person who was knowledgeable in futures trading was

the young Chief Economist for the Chicago Board of

Trade, Doctor Richard Sandor. He remains my friend, and I

did a little work for him recently.

Since I was knowledgeable in this new area of law,

my fellow Georgian, President Jimmy Carter (for whose

winning campaign I had worked) offered to appoint me

Chairman of the new commission. Unfortunately, I needed

to earn more money in the private sector because my first

wife was terminally ill. Therefore, President Carter

appointed James Stone Chairman of the CFTC. Stone was

noted for two things: One, he had written a book titled,

"One Way for Wall Street," and two, he married the widow

of Supreme Court Justice William Douglas. Unfortunately,

he has not up to the pressure of heading a regulatory

agency. He had a nervous breakdown and had to take leave

of absence.

I remember discussing this with my friend Barbara Holum, the Legislative Liaison of the CFTC. Later, in the Clinton administration, Barbara was appointed to be an CFTC commissioner in her own right.

As for me, I co-founded the little law firm, Davis & McLeod. Our first client was the Chicago Board of Trade (CBOT). CBOT remained my client until it merged into the Chicago Mercantile Exchange (CME) in 2008. After that, I served in a pro bono capacity under CFTC Chairman Gary Gensler as we worked on the Dodd-Frank amendments.

Gensler was at the center of dealing with the 2008 financial crises, which involved the $400 trillion over-the-counter derivatives or swaps market. This legislation is known as *Dodd-Frank*, but the correct name is "The Wall Street Reform Consumer Protection Act of 2010". Chairman Gensler's role in lobbying Congress to give him the adequate statutory authority to do his job was not revealed in any official documents. In January, 2010, he engineered the formation of the Commodity Markets Oversight Coalition and the Americans for Financial Reform Coalition.

I know all of this because I was a member of these coalitions and I helped in arranging meetings with Congress. Gensler would meet with us on a weekly basis. The titular head of the coalition was a hedge fund manager domiciled in the US Virgin Islands with an office in Atlanta. However, Gensler met with us every week and was our real leader.

I also recall that the current Presidential contender, Elizabeth Warren, was a participant in that coalition. Having lost my savings, I don't have the funds to contribute much to her campaign, but I have offered to do what I can on financial issues. I believe that she is the only candidate who has expertise in this area of government issues.

I was able to participate on a pro bono basis because I had recently lost my representation in the Chicago Board of Trade after the Chicago Mercantile Exchange acquired

in 2008. I remained a part of the Coalition until I was

hired by old friend John Damgard, President of the Futures

Industry Association. I remained there until he retired about

two years ago.

Unfortunately, the current leadership of the CFTC

has not shown the same kind of strength that it exuded

when Gensler was in command. The CFTC is allowing one

large clearing member, INT FCStone, to get away with

shifting responsibility for hundreds of millions of dollars of

losses from themselves to innocent investors. I have

repeatedly pointed out that without the integrity of its

clearing members, futures trading on exchanges does not

work.

Moreover, it was only a few years prior to this, in 2013,

that the CFTC fined INT FCStone $1.5 million and forced

them to bear a loss of $127 million. After the OptionSellers

meltdown in the second week of November 2018, the

CFTC took a polar opposite approach. OptionSellers was only the introducing broker who persuaded investors to put up their money. All trades were made and cleared by INT FCStone. Not only was there no fine in this 2018 case, but the CFTC allowed INT FCStone to bill innocent investors for the losses. Despite numerous Freedom of Information Act requests, I have been unable to find out why they have taken this position. I have also been unable to ascertain how many millions of dollars were lost. I have written some blogs on my website to address these issues. I have pointed out that without the integrity of the clearing members of the commodity exchanges, the system does not work.

I am not blaming the new chairman of the CFTC, Heath Tarbutin, because he has just taken office. I have told him that I was going to write a book about this debacle because I have exhausted all my appeals and gotten no relief. However, it is clear to me that someone in the

agency succumbed to improper influence by INT FCStone.

As we found out in the case of Watergate, the

coverup is often worse than the crime. When I worked for

the Senate Agriculture Committee during the Watergate

scandal, this drama played out in the Senate Caucus Room,

which was next to the Senate Agriculture Committee suite

where I worked. Our Conference room was used as a

holding room for the public hearings next door. My boss,

Senator Talmadge, was a member of Watergate Committee.

We did not do any work during the hearings. I do

remember that a pretty young reporter named Lesly Stahl

got her start covering the Watergate proceedings. I still like

to see her on the CBS "60 Minutes," every Sunday evening.

For a few years, I was a partner in the law firm

Scott, Harrison & McLeod. The "Scott" was Senator Hugh

Scott, formerly the Republican leader of the Senate. When

the House was planning to impeach President Richard

Nixon, Senator Scott advised Nixon that if the House impeached him, the Senate would convict him. With that, Nixon left town. He did not return until the funeral of my great friend Hubert Humphrey, who laid in state in the Capitol Rotunda. As I recounted in my book, "The Death of Civility and Common Sense," Humphrey called Nixon and asked him to attend his funeral. I was honored to get a call from Humphrey in the week before he died, but his call was more of a pep talk to me and said nothing about death or a funeral. Along with a multitude of other people Nixon did come, the first time he had returned to Washington since he had left in disgrace.

Current Lawsuits

Several lawsuits are pending on behalf of victimized investors. Perhaps the most active law firm in this is the Chapman Albin firm in Ohio. While this is an excellent law firm, investors should not have to rely on law firms that charge clients contingency fees of at least thirty five percent of what is recovered. This is what the taxpayers are paying the CFTC over $300 million a year to do. Moreover, if this were under the jurisdiction of the SEC, it would already have been done.

The final chapter of this book has not been written. I still have some hope the CFTC will do its job. Perhaps if it has to answer to Congress, it will do so. I have encouraged investors and their attorneys, on my blog, to petition their members of Congress. You may see this on my website.

Each State has two Senators, and voters know who they are. If their members are on the Senate Committee on Agriculture, Nutrition, and Forestry, it is even more important. This is the committee that has jurisdiction over the CFTC and the Committee where I served as General Counsel and Staff director. However, even if this is not the case, the Senate is a very collegial body and they talk with each other frequently. I hope investors who were victims will call their Senators.

Thus far, I have found no interest in the House of Representatives in helping victims of OptionSellers/INT FCStone. The committee that has jurisdiction is the House Agriculture Committee. The members of this committee can readily be found by going online. I would encourage every victimized investor to contact his or her member of Congress.

I am an optimist who believes in our system of government. I believe that when the final chapter is written, it will document

that we have prevailed.

I have written a few blogs on the subject of

allowing INT FCStone to escape the

disastrous meltdown

of OptionSellers.com without any

consequences for itself. This is the first time

in the history of futures trading that this has

happened. The futures markets have always

relied on the integrity of the clearing

members to make the system work.

Make no mistake, OptionSellers was only the trading advisor for the clients that it signed up. INT FCstone was the clearing member who placed the trades on the futures markets. They guaranteed that" all of the transactions are either hedges or contemplate actual delivery and receipt of the property and payment therefor".

This is absolutely the opposite of what OptionSellers was doing, as described in their book and all of their promotional literature. It is clear that they were only using INT IFSone to sell naked put options

to collect the premiums. They never were
hedges and there was never an expectation
that actual delivery would be made. Their
strategy was their expectation that these
options would expire worthless and they
would simply pocket the premiums.

No executives of INT FCstone can testify in
a court of law that they were unaware of this
without committing perjury.

I received the following letter dated
December 14, 2018 from Laura Riso ,
Victim Specialist of the FBI, December 14,

2018. It says that I have been identified as

the victim of a crime.

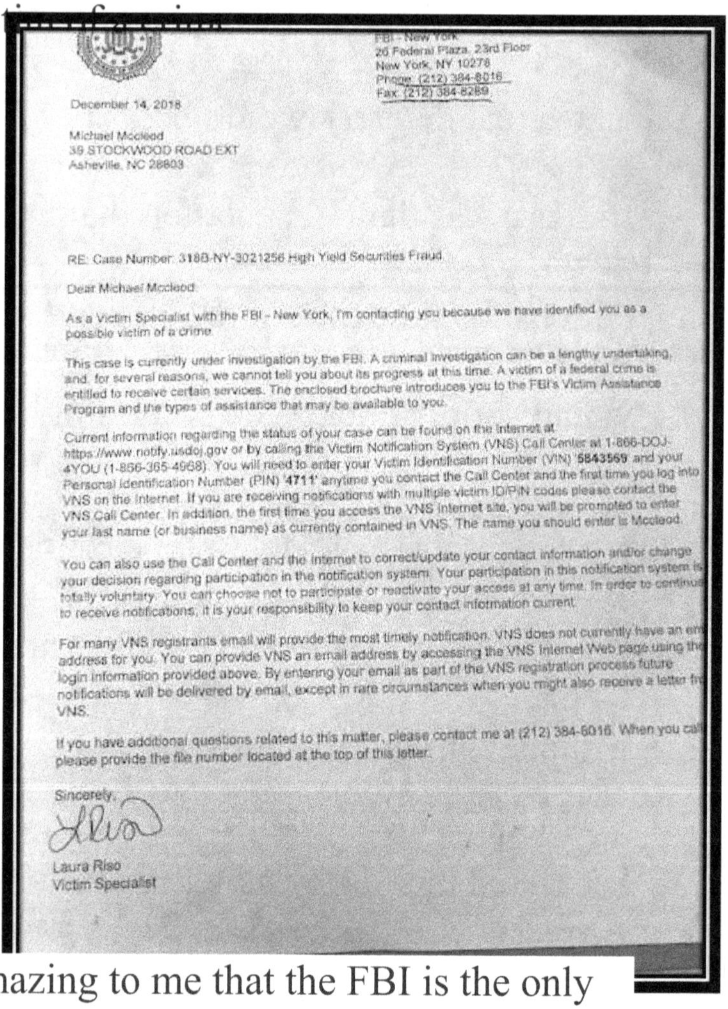

FBI - New York
26 Federal Plaza, 23rd Floor
New York, NY 10278
Phone: (212) 384-8016
Fax: (212) 384-8289

December 14, 2018

Michael Mccleod
39 STOCKWOOD ROAD EXT
Asheville, NC 28803

RE: Case Number: 318B-NY-3021256 High Yield Securities Fraud

Dear Michael Mccleod:

As a Victim Specialist with the FBI – New York, I'm contacting you because we have identified you as a possible victim of a crime.

This case is currently under investigation by the FBI. A criminal investigation can be a lengthy undertaking, and, for several reasons, we cannot tell you about its progress at this time. A victim of a federal crime is entitled to receive certain services. The enclosed brochure introduces you to the FBI's Victim Assistance Program and the types of assistance that may be available to you.

Current information regarding the status of your case can be found on the Internet at https://www.notify.usdoj.gov or by calling the Victim Notification System (VNS) Call Center at 1-866-DOJ-4YOU (1-866-365-4968). You will need to enter your Victim Identification Number (VIN) '5843569' and your Personal Identification Number (PIN) '4711' anytime you contact the Call Center and the first time you log into VNS on the Internet. If you are receiving notifications with multiple victim ID/PIN codes please contact the VNS Call Center. In addition, the first time you access the VNS Internet site, you will be prompted to enter your last name (or business name) as currently contained in VNS. The name you should enter is Mccleod.

You can also use the Call Center and the Internet to correct/update your contact information and/or change your decision regarding participation in the notification system. Your participation in this notification system is totally voluntary. You can choose not to participate or reactivate your access at any time. In order to continue to receive notifications, it is your responsibility to keep your contact information current.

For many VNS registrants email will provide the most timely notification. VNS does not currently have an email address for you. You can provide VNS an email address by accessing the VNS Internet Web page using the login information provided above. By entering your email as part of the VNS registration process future notifications will be delivered by email, except in rare circumstances when you might also receive a letter from VNS.

If you have additional questions related to this matter, please contact me at (212) 384-8016. When you call please provide the file number located at the top of this letter.

Sincerely,

Laura Riso
Victim Specialist

It is amazing to me that the FBI is the only

federal agency that has any interest in

helping me while the CFTC has done

nothing. Congress should look at either merging the CFTC into the SEC or at least give the SEC jurisdiction over all options trading. That should include trading of options on commodities as well as on stocks.

Michael R. McLeod

www.ingramcontent.com/pod-product-compliance
Lightning Source LLC
Chambersburg PA
CBHW061553250726
48657CB00006B/2480